My Creature

BY JACK PRELUTSKY

CREATURES BY Anthony Lucas

PHOTOGRAPHY BY Malcolm Cross

HOUGHTON MIFFLIN COMPANY

BOSTON

ATLANTA   DALLAS   GENEVA, ILLINOIS   PALO ALTO   PRINCETON

I made a creature

out of clay,

just what it is

is hard to say.

Its neck is thin,

its legs are fat,

it's like a bear

and like a bat.

It's like a snake

and like a snail,

it has a little

curly tail,

a shaggy mane,

a droopy beard,

its ears are long,

its smile is weird.

It has four horns,

one beady eye,

two floppy wings

(though it can't fly),

it only sits

upon my shelf—

just think, I made it by myself!